MW01012244

What if You'd Met
Beethoven?

by Carrie Mieko Myers

Copyright © 2004 by Scholastic Inc.
All rights reserved. Published by Scholastic Inc.
Printed in the U.S.A.

ISBN 0-439-69713-1

SCHOLASTIC and associated logos and designs are trademarks and/or registered trademarks of Scholastic Inc.

15   40   16 15

SCHOLASTIC INC.
New York Toronto London Auckland Sydney
Mexico City New Delhi Hong Kong Buenos Aires

Ludwig van Beethoven was a famous composer. A composer writes music. Beethoven wrote music for the piano, the violin, voice, and orchestra.

Beethoven lived over 200 years ago. He was born in Germany. But most of the time, he lived in Austria.

Do you want to know something amazing? Beethoven was deaf! He started to lose his hearing when he was still a young man.

Can you imagine writing and playing music with no hearing?

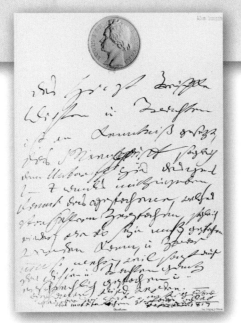

Beethoven's handwriting

If you wanted to talk to Beethoven, you would write your words and questions down and let him read them. Then he would answer out loud.

What if you could meet Beethoven? What questions would you ask him? Pretend you are interviewing Beethoven, or asking him questions, as you read along.

Beethoven's father

Your question: How did you become a musician?

Beethoven: My father wanted me to be a famous piano player. I started music lessons when I was four years old. I studied with many great musicians.

When I was 8, I played in public for the first
time. I often played for counts and countesses.

I also learned to write music. I published
my first piece of music when I was 12! I was
very excited.

Beethoven used an "ear trumpet" to help him hear better.

What happened to your hearing?

Beethoven: When I was 18, my ears started to buzz and ring. If someone shouted, my ears hurt.

I went to many doctors, but none of them could help. Now, I can't hear voices or music. But I can still compose, or write, my music.

How do you write music since you can't hear?

Beethoven: I can still hear music in my head. I write down what I hear. I can write a whole symphony in my head!

What's a symphony?

Beethoven: A symphony is a long piece of music for an orchestra.

An orchestra is a big group of musicians. They play many different instruments.

flute

trumpet

violin

piano

How do you write a symphony?

Beethoven: Each instrument in an orchestra has a different sound.

I decide what notes each instrument plays. Then I write the notes down.

notes

staff

What do notes look like when you write them down?

Beethoven: You write notes on a group of lines and spaces called a staff. Each line or space matches a different pitch. A pitch is how high or low the note sounds.

sheet music

Some notes look round and hollow (whole notes). Some look like they are waving flags (eighth or sixteenth notes). The way a note looks shows the musician how fast to play it.

A whole page of notes is called sheet music.

When do you write music?

Beethoven: I get up very early in the morning. I write until lunchtime. Sometimes I take a break and go for a walk. But I still hear the music in my head!

I would like to write my own music! Do you have any advice?

Beethoven: Practice your instrument. Learn from great musicians.

And always listen to the music in your head!

The End

Glossary

Composer — Someone who writes music.

Orchestra — A large group of musicians.

Pitch — How high or low a note sounds.

Sheet music — Pieces of paper with music written on them.

Staff — A group of lines and spaces that notes are written on.

Symphony — A long musical piece played by an orchestra. Each symphony has at least three or four parts, called movements.